How to personalize this book for your Dear Granddaughter!

Original cover

Tools needed: (all are available at a scrapbook supply store and/or craft store)

- Acid-free glue stick
- Photo mounting squares/tape
- Scissors or photo trimmer
- Fine point writing pen (acid-free, light-fast, waterproof, fade-proof, smear-proof and non-bleeding)
- Acid-free paper for writing additional notes/letters

Dear Friends,

As a grandparent, you have the precious gifts of history to share with your granddaughter — memories of your own life plus wisdom and dreams for hers. Using our book as your "canvas," you can embellish as much or as little as you wish, creating a keepsake your granddaughter will cherish forever. Some ways to personalize:

Cover personalized with photo

Customize the cover photo

Slip out the cover insert and paste your special photo in the indicated area.

Page personalized with photos, journaling and colored paper

Affix your photos over ours!

One of the easiest ways to make this book your own is to gather your favorite photos and adhere them over the ones we show. Some spaces are a traditional 4 x 6 size; others are circular or sub-sized. For the cleanest cuts, you would want to use a photo trimmer (see above).

Page personalized with photo and journaling

Record "guided" memories

With our guided journal pages, you can share fond memories from a time your granddaughter will never know. Perhaps she will discover much in common with her grandmother!

Page personalized with memento (fortune) and journaling

Share your wisdom

What words of wisdom would you like to share with your granddaughter? You can certainly add your anecdotes to any page. We have, however, built in a special page for grandmother's wisdom.

Page personalized with photos, memorabelia and journaling

Capture the spirit of your granddaughter

Do you see in your grandchild a budding musician? Is she a book or animal lover? Celebrate how you see her by creating a page about her with photos, mementos, and musings.

Dear Granddaughter

a message of Love

by
Marianne Richmond

sourcebooks

Dear Granddaughter
a message of Love

Library of Congress Control Number: 2006909244

Text and Illustrations © 2008 Marianne Richmond Studios, Inc.
Cover and internal design © 2010 Sourcebooks, Inc.

Published by Sourcebooks, Inc.
P.O. Box 4410
Naperville, IL 60567-4410
www.sourcebooks.com

Illustrations by Marianne Richmond

Book design by Sara Dare Biscan

Printed in China
LEO 10 9 8 7 6 5 4 3 2

This book is dedicated to beloved granddaughters everywhere, especially Julia and Lily — MR

A gifted author and illustrator, Marianne Richmond lives in Minneapolis, MN with her husband, four children and one dog.

Marianne shares her unique spirit and enchanting artwork in her other titles:

The Gift of an Angel
The Gift of a Memory
Hooray for You!,
The Gifts of Being Grand
I Love You So...
Dear Daughter
Dear Son
Dear Grandson
My Shoes Take Me Where I Want to Go
Fish Kisses and Gorilla Hugs

Marianne continues to create products that help people connect with those who mean the most to them. Her repertoire includes books, stationery and giftware.

Pages are acid free

Dear

Love,

Date

Nobody can do for children what grandparents do. Grandparents sort of sprinkle stardust over the lives of children. —Alex Haley

DEAR *Granddaughter,*

You **truly** are a dear granddaughter.

Cherished beyond measure.

How **Blessed**

I am to have
the gift of you
in my life.

While I have been here since the first second of **you** —

I have lived many years as me!

Can you imagine your grandmother as a baby? A young girl? Or as a teenager?

There are a few things I'd like to **share** with you about **my life**, just in case you ever find yourself wishing you knew.

Certificate of Birth

My full name

That name was chosen because

I was born

date

location

I weighed

weight

length

My parents names

Brothers and sisters

My family lived on this street

in this town

I remember my neighborhood as...

As a young girl...

My chores included

I went to school at

My favorite things to do with my friends were

Some of my favorite things were

Sports

Foods

Colors

School Subjects

Friends

And as a young Lady...

I graduated in   from

After I finished school, I

My first job was

I began to date at the age of

I met your grandfather at

we went on dates to

I was   years old
and he was

We were married on

I liked him because

in the year of

I remember the
first time I held you,
and the **instant**,
all Consuming,

giGanTiC

love I felt.

I celebrated your every
accomplishment,
big and small.

As I watch **You** grow,
I am in awe of the **amazing**,
beautiful young lady you are.

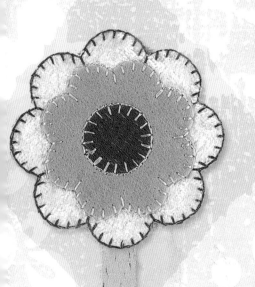

Time after time,
you touch my heart
with your affection,
your playfulness,
and your
extraordinary
individuality.

The things I **especially** appreciate about you are:

I love being your **grand** mother, because my job is great joy — loving you, spoiling you, playing with you... and encouraging you.

(I can happily leave the discipline stuff up to your parents!)

SPECIAL MOMENTS
MOMENTS

My favorite moments
with you are...

In my life,
I have always loved to.

DREAM BIG DREAMS
BELIEVE
THEY'LL COME TRUE

and
have felt
passionate
about...

In **Your** journey through Life, I want you to discover exactly who **you** are — your talents, your passions, your goals and your dreams...

that appears at regular inte.
entric *journal* >
syn magazine, newspaper, organ, periodical, review
journey *n* passing or a passage from one place to another
<at that time it was a four day *journey* from Boston to
New York> <she was tired though their *journey* was barely
begun >
syn expedition, peregrination(s), travel(s), trek, trip; *com-*
pare TRIP 1
rel excursion, jaunt, junket, sally, tour; cruise, voyage;
pilgrimage, progress, safari
journey *vb syn* GO 1, fare, hie, pass, proceed, ‖process,
push on, repair, travel, wend
jovial *adj syn* MERRY blith⸺ blithcsome, festive, gay,

JOURNEY

AND to have the

CHANCE

to design a life

that

Celebrates

your

WONDERFUL

un🔘queness

As my precious **grand-**daughter, I wish you memorable moments,

forever kind of friendships, and the **opportunity** to serve others.

Believe it or not, I was young once, too.

I went through "phases." Made poor choices. Had my heart broken and my feelings hurt. Disappointed my parents. Let down a friend.

I survived and (usually) learned from my experiences.

How else could I gain my grandmotherly wisdom?

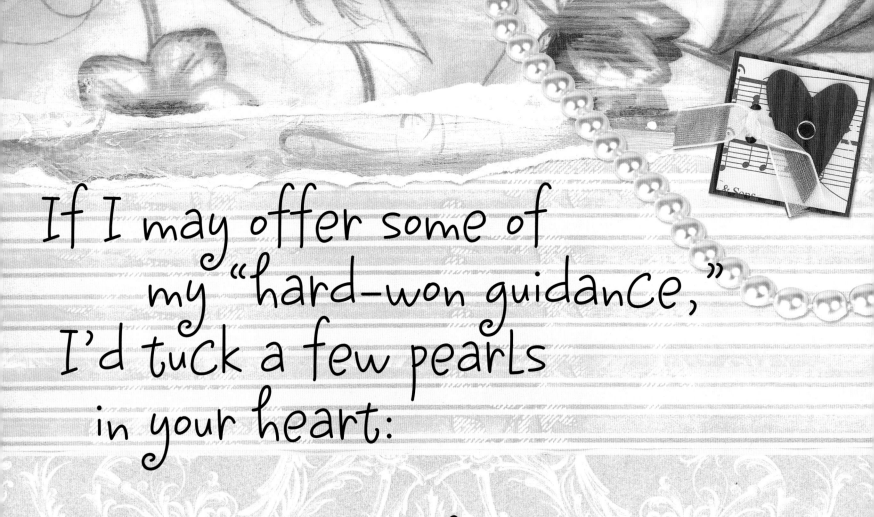

If I may offer some of
my "hard-won guidance,"
I'd tuck a few pearls
in your heart:

Forgive... even if you
can't forget.

Be honest,
even if it's tough to do.

Use white toilet paper.

Imagine yourself in another's shoes to gain understanding.

Oh, and a couple other thoughts...

I wish I could **guarantee** you a trouble-free trip through life. But, grandmothers don't fib.

What I can tell you, however, is that struggles make you stronger, smarter, and more sensitive to others.

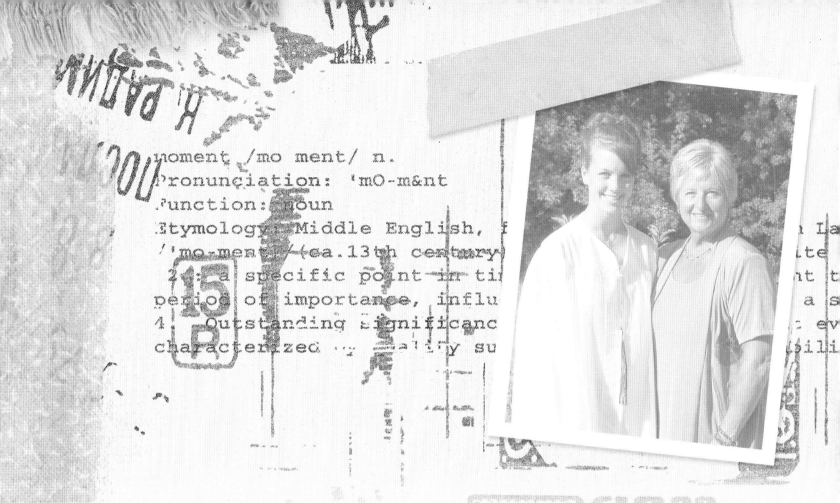

moment /mo ment/ n.
Pronunciation: 'mO-m&nt
Function: noun
Etymology: Middle English, f
'mo-ment / (ca.13th century)
2 : a specific point in ti
period of importance, influ
4 : Outstanding significanc
characterized ...

They also encourage you
to welcome joy with
outstretched arms — and
with a thankful heart.
And this is all good.

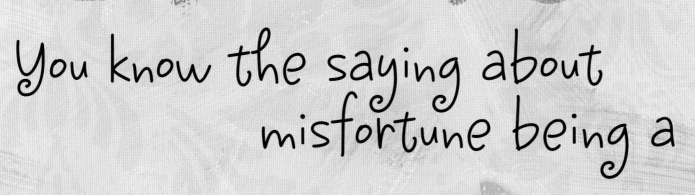

You know the saying about
misfortune being a

"blessing in disguise?"...

It can be true, I promise.

My **hope**, dear one,
is that when you
think about your
grandmother,
you think of her with

PrIDe

Love and

ADMIRATION

As I do about
you,
my dear,

dear
granddaughter.